Notes of Defiance

A Fanfare in Common Cause

SONTAGE CHAPBOOK 3
2026

# Contents

Editor's Notes

So now it's 2026, and I'm back to being an Editor.

None of these writings have been edited for content.

Opinions expressed are completely by the authors.

We are aware our dissident voices are now particularly important to publicize because the administration of our country is hell bent on rewriting history. And when that pendulum swings back to some form of real history, we want our side of events available!

Another thing we Sontagers recognize, is the extreme rapidity of change of headlines of current events. Many of the items I mentioned in The Daily Spew poem are passé and have lost their urgency.

And **We The People** — *we Sontagers wish to state we do not condone the criminal actions on our lives, and the pursuit of every person's free speech.*

We wish everyone love, peace, security and comfort.

And SPEAK OUT!

Thanks to Brian Meyer for for-
matting the layout, and providing
the illustrations!

**Extreme Appreciation Tendered to the
Mission Hills – Hillcrest Branch Library**
215 W Washington St. San Diego, CA 92103
(619) 692-4910
for the use of its facilities.
For information and calendar see:
https://www.sandiego.gov/public-library/locations/mission-hills-library
Particular thanks to Stephen Wheeler
for his assistance with our meetings.
(And also to their fabulous Bookstore!)

Mark A. Ardagna

Biography

Mark was born in Kansas City, Missouri. He learned to tie his shoes on the car trip from Kansas City to San Diego when his family moved to California. He was five. After awhile he became very good at it. He continues tying them to this day.

Mark was among the students of the first graduating class in 1964 at Castle Park High School.

At Southwestern College he was a member of the Rattlesnake Patrol. He wrote term papers for students who didn't or couldn't write them for themselves. He almost got caught when he submitted a term a paper he had written to an instructor who had just received the same paper from another student.

Mark went to San Diego State College but left after his house burned down in 1969. He hitched a ride to Washington D.C. He was first published in Woodwind magazine in Washington. He was paid in copies.

He was a scuba diver from 1964 until he was hit by a large Tiger Shark near the Imperial Beach Pier. He didn't go back into the water again for twenty years. He always said it was not because of that shark attack but it probably was.

Mark went back to school at SDSU. He completed his B.S. in Biology, a B.A. in English and an M.A. in Creative Writing. He challenged Greek I and II and was awarded an A in Greek I and a B in Greek II. He volunteered at Disabled Student Services for several years and tutored students, especially veterans. He was elected to Alpha Mu Gamma, the language Honors Society, Phi Beta Kappa, and was honored as a council elected Life Member of the Alumni Association.

He studied with Don Miguel Angel Ruiz before he was a "Don." He also studied with Earl, a Native American Medicine Man. He volunteered at the Natural History Museum and is an expert on meteorites.

Mark outlived three wives: Chris, Marci and Carrie. All three of them died from cancer. He really doesn't believe it was his fault.

He lives in Southwestern Chula Vista with his sister Mary, his three little boys, Ivan, Dewey and Jake, his little girl Frankie and niece Lucy. He has a Tiny Library and a "Take a Rock, Leave a Rock" display in front of his house from which he derives great pleasure.

Mark belongs to South Bay Scribes and Sontage and likes to write.

Words Like Bullets
Mark Ardagna

My words like bullets
Slam into the hide of the
World's enemy

But instead of hurting him
They fall like pieces of paper
To the ground

And are trampled into the dirt
As though they never
Existed.

They form a mat
As thick as cardboard for
The monster.

My only hope
Is that the paper
Pieces

Would trip up the monster
But that cannot happen.
A monster

Who lives in dirt and mud
Cannot be tripped up
By it

Even if he is badly smeared by it.
Mud is Mud. Even if it talks
Like People.

Trumping Trump
Mark Ardagna

To trump someone is to use a specially
designated card to win a hand or trick.

Older understanding was to devise fraud-
ulently, to concoct or counterfeit.

Trumpery means showy or worthless,
nonsense, rubbish: showy but valueless.

Middle English trumpery from Old French
tromperie from tromper to cheat.

Someone in the family wanted to be
known by the name of Trump.

It identified some kind of power they
thought they had. The word "trump"

Has not generally thought to be clean
and wholesome. You play a card and

win the pot but wait a minute, the next
person trumps you. Let's face it card

games are competitive and tend to draw
people with questionable mores to them.

Sometimes a person who is used to
winning at card games gets into politics.

They expect the real world to work just
like the card games they are used to
winning.

D.T. Rump
Mark Ardagna

D.T. Rump hitched up his white horse

Scratched his pug nose

Hitched his trousers high enough

To show off his pedigree

And rode into the night

A century late yelling:

The Arabs and Jews

Intellectuals and clerks

Progressives and Democrats

Are coming

Dumpity Trump
Mark Ardagna

Dumpity Trump, dumpity Trump,
Dumpity Trump, dump Trump

Dumpity Trump,
dumpity Trump
Dumpity Trump,
dump Trump

Dumpity Trump, dumpity Trump,
Dumpity Trump, dump Trump

Dumpity Trump

Dumpity Trump, dump Trump

Someone Said
Mark Ardagna

Someone said that Christ approved of

Donald Trump. I thought about that

and thought it odd that Christ would

approve of the Anti-Christ

Still, looking at the history of Christianity,

2000 years of hatred, plunder and murder,

from the days of Constantine to the

Crusades

To the 16th century Spanish priests in

Mexico, Europeans in North America

To India to Africa on down to the Nazis,

The French

In Viet Nam and a thousand other times

and places, perhaps Christ came back as

Donald Trump. And 2000 years of Christian

History

Show that Donald Trump accepts a history

as brutal as this and because of it he will do

Whatever the hell he wants.

The Tempering of the Populace
Mark Ardagna

We are steel plunged into cold

After being heated to cherry red.

We are being tempered each day.

Tempered.

The daily news. Tempered. We

Will not shatter when we are dropped.

Each story makes us stronger.

By stronger

Is meant that we react less and less

to each story that comes along.

We are tempered by each assault

On our heart.

We will not shatter! We are tempered!

We will listen to stories that would

Have outraged us before and not

Care a bit.

Karen Waters-Montijo

Biography

Karen Waters-Montijo makes her home in rural San Diego. She is retired after many years working in community and public health, and now has the luxury of spending time with her family, friends, and books.

The Party
Karen Waters-Montijo

It's a skillset I have as an administrator:
Planning, assigning, writing reports that no one
reads.
But I'm retired, with no outlet for such finely honed
abilities,
and I wondered if God might have tasks for an aide,
of sorts,
to organize a gathering of women, in a grand arena,
perhaps a ballroom,
decorated with large urns of roses at each table,
and freesias at every seat,
the scents intoxicating to all the guests.

No dress code required for the event:

Bring your newly-filled bee-stung lips,

low-cut dresses with tatas out to there, and

heavy false eyelashes to bat like a silent movie actress in her

close-up.

Or wear natural grey hair, once thick, but now limp

with prescription meds permeating the roots,

sensible shoes, a bit of gloss, long tunics that hide the waist.

Young women in tight black ensembles, pierced and hip,

or in frilly blouses buttoned to the neck,

or wrapped in fabrics handed down through time from

ancestors.

All are beautiful.

All are afraid that freedom will demand too much, or not

enough.

All are afraid to be alone, afraid of settling.

All are welcome in this haven, away from predators, liars,

prevaricators,

and gaslighters,

where we toss the agenda and buzz around each other

with the excitement of bees in a patch of rosemary flowers

drinking in nectar, as understanding dawns, excitement grows.

Women coalesce to create a secret service for their hearts

as minds expand around each other.

The earth knows something is up, trembling

with the knowledge that it will be saved, at last.

Brian Meyer

Brian Meyer is a plein air poet and painter in jazz. Known for creating on the spot art at local concerts and clubs in his native San Diego. His words and art arise from these moments; a practice based on jazz improvisation, developing chops outside of any comfort zone, and always asking; does this swing?

A member of the San Diego Watercolor Society, where he displays his art, and a regular at monthly paint-outs for over 10 years. These are led by Lorri Lynch on the second Saturday of each month. As Lorri always says, "If you don't go, you don't grow."

His art is about the community, and you will find him out and about in San Diego working plein air at the beach, trying to "catch" some waves in a painting, in Hillcrest at a coffee shop sketching and writing, or up in the Laguna Mountains painting trees.

Many know him from being handed "random acts of art", a sketch of people just being themselves, because art matters, because being seen matters.

Brian is a US Army Veteran. He served in Desert Storm as a combat signaler for 16th Corps Support Group.

You can order his books via Amazon:
Towers Between
The Politics of Hell
Resistance isn't Poetry
Song of the Forest

a watercolor
by george

it says

her
by george   sand
the writer
a chosen   name
taken from   another man
a pseudonym   of fiction
to free   her words
against   this world
made only   for me
now   hanging
for perpetuity   on museum walls
a fiction   named sand

the woman
who had   to file for
a permit   to wear
mens clothing
who smoked   tobacco
who strode free   in circles
only made   for men
who wrote   subversively
whose novels   were more popular
than victor hugo   or balzac
who just did   her thing
who never
was just   a writer
but a painter   and a critic
an activist   and a political strategist
lauded never   as a woman
but only   in terms of man

I see   her hand
long after   her passing
these colors   granulate
this ultramarine has grayed
this paper   faded into yellow
leaving me   to imagine
its former   vibrancy
this debris   of her
doing

                 her thing
her art   still doing
                 its thing
her art   still demanding
even as   time erodes
her art   into sand

I found it   abandoned
an old   discarded chisel
never loved   never truly used
mass produced   never true
an ignorant edge   gleaming
but brittle   to adversity
quickly   its tip
too dull   to trust
given up   to rust

its iron
soaking up   its tears
into   reddish
rust encrusted   fears

I start   by cleaning
this rusted   soul
bathing her   in oil
my wire brush   revealing
that naked   black iron below
I ask   "is there enough
                       of you left?"
she replies   "I don't know"

my whetstones   caress
as I guide   her back
watching   how it wears
testing   her metal
swirls   and patterns reveal
polished   funhouse mirrors
distorting   the real
I teach   her iron
those parts   high
eagerly   learn
until flat   she lies

only then   its tip
I flatten   it
a true edge   is where
two sides   are square
no longer   arguing
each   is defining
true sharpness   be
when opposing sides   agree

this chisel   now mine
her wounds   and scars
reflect not   her worth
but   our neglect
how we see   is not demanding
our hands   must hone
our guide   to understanding

they abandoned us
as changelings in the forest

they thought we could
not feel
we could not talk
so they left their children
left their babies
to die alone

that the fey folk
replaced us
replaced us with stones

now the world
has forgotten how
to feel

we treat sensitivity
as insanity

these tears as a man
just weakness

gotta be productive
we got online dating
first dates are now
job interviews

will you work out

we blame   autism
on refrigerator moms
then on   vaccines
was it   mercury?
secret   additives?
processed   food?
                 tylenol?
better to get   measles
than computer   chips
that   track us

I am   your conspiracy
I am   your mythology
I am   a changeling
I am   of the forest
I am   autistic
I am   of the silent ones
I may   be quiet
I don't feel on the outside
but inside   where its real
I feel

             I feel

every beast
has a mother
who loves him or her

despite the darkness
even nightmares have brothers

I close my eyes
without light I see
what each eternity
of sleep reveals

family feeds our hunger
for each other

the way we hurt
is why we hurt
each other

our pain defines us
our fear it drives us

just more reasons
to hurt each other

our pain we reveal
we make this beast
we make it real

what I awaken
I dream of demons
this

is me

even beasts need love

this countries   enemies
the confederacy   the axis of old

the new axis   of evil
the authoritarian   the dictator
of illiberal   democracy

now arguing   the third reich
did   good things

that fellow   americans
are intolerant   for judging
that   sieg heil

we are   the bigots
for   not seeing
that diversity   is divisive
that equality   divides
that excluding   that segregation
is a fundamental   right
that history   should
comfort   and reinforce
that we   should all
look   alike

the psychopath   does not believe
in love   and kindness
the bigot   and racist
does not   believe in difference

all that   threatens
white   pride
our racism   disguised

hey nazi
a word we cannot say

those four letter words
the f word
the n word
the c word
that triple k

used to be
bigots had to hide

to wear a hood

they had to shut up

to speak their views
left them banished
unemployed exiles

we conflate our words
we call war genocide
we call those we disagree with
fascist and nazi

in using a word
to describe
every thing

it's a lot like cussing

your meaning
isn't in the words
but in your rage
and anger

we reduced   nazi
to just   another
four   letter word
an empty   adjective
for whatever   we object to

not some   moral
high   ground
we once   all agreed
was   evil

but   contempt
just   another
word   for them

when maga   showed up
and fit   the definition
no one   listened

archaeologists know
this past revealed
what we call history
is never what we tell ourselves
this what we wanted
or what we buried

we argue with biography
we bury the bones
of our story

of what is written
what remains

but this what
that remains

what

is found

artifacts speak
more than myth
more than testimony
more than the beliefs we live
but to the reality of how we died
of how we met
our destiny

we elect these leaders
on the claim
there is no good
in government
and wonder why
they prove it true

this attitude corrupts

hidden by this criticism
we elect contempt
those against the government
see it only as a business
that politics is we the people
being bought and sold

the bully pulpit now bullies us
it plays us like a fiddle
politics as religion
the dear leader
replacing god
ever the chosen one
above right and wrong

no longer a democracy
of we the people
but a republic
this we now ruled
by lust and power

never leaders that inspire
never leaders who reveal
the good in government
when it is we
we the people
who no longer believe

Charlie Berigan

Biography

Charlie Berigan is a rabid enthusiast for many arts: Music, Literature, Art, Theatre and Film. He has been professionally active in several of them; initially obtaining degrees from the San Francisco Conservatory of Music and the Juilliard School. His teachers included John Adams and Earl Wild. He has been involved in the theatre as performer, musical director, composer. He's worked on projects ranging from the Blitzstein "The Cradle Will Rock"to Brecht/Weill's "Three Penny Opera" to other Shakespeare, Brecht, Marivaux, Beaumarchais, Caryl Churchill, Ronald Ribman plays, not to overlook the Topsy-Turvydom of Messrs. Gilbert and Sullivan. He enjoys writing and sharing that writing and has contributed numerous times to the San Diego Poetry Annual. He is a member of both the "South Bay Scribes" and the Mission Hills "Sontage".

Again Obama: Really?
Charlie Berigan

I don't get the hatred, the bile, the resentment
Is it his smarts, or maybe his class?
Can't be his color; don't be an ass—
At one point the nation will wake up and see
Donald Defraud on display, an insult to history.
Between you and me, this Prez DJT—
The worst of the worst in our living memory
At some point he'll stumble, at some point he'll fall
We'll be there and eager, for that judgment call.

1600 Penn At Present
Charlie Berigan

Grumbily bumbily bimbily bowe
The White House is all screwed up, you know
Hibbily bibbily battley boo
Present day Prezzie quite the moron, it's true
Lumbidy dumbidy he's got no plan
East Wing's just rubble now—take a good scan
Why not go full Pharoah—a Pyramid's nice
Ballroom, Casino…what matter the price?
He's out of control, of that I've no doubt
How'd we ever end up with such an obvious lout?

Show Biz Sentinels
Charlie Berigan

He's done it now—
our Toddler in Chief
Hubris completely
running wild
Declaring war
on those Jesters of the Night
Not in any way
comprehending
the drip drip drip
of the blood that's drawn
by their pointed barbs
will in the end
define his 'brand'
Let me put this
just like this, Mr. POTUS:
the boob tube made you
and now, that same device
could end your farce
and Colbert, Kimmel
Fallon and Stewart
be just the sort of
apocalypse horsemen
to trample you, Donald
right into the dust.

Top Gun Donald: "Bombs Away"
Charlie Berigan

Of course, as soon as I heard

I had to have a look…

After all, the man has

his daily outrage quota to be met

And this exceeded

all previous transgression benchmark—

Never in our narrative

has a sitting Chief Executive

shown such brazen, naked

contempt for a public…

Forget the comic coronets

and the soundscape sampled

without artist permission

This message is clear:

He's simply without fear

of judgment, accountability

any and all sense of

possible moral or legal restraint

Pictures truly are worth

many words quite potent

and this mad gesture of obscenity

speaks of gravest danger

to our country, our people

not to overlook the world.

Spirit Of Stormtrooper Past
Charlie Berigan

Imaging my surprise
when scrolling about the 'net…
Some joker referenced old 'Horst Wessel'—
Of course I knew the story, man, and tune
In point of fact, my troubled mind
had already made bold 'leap of faith'
But I'd kinda cast it aside
thinking: "Ach, isn't this just a bit far fetched?"
But apparently someone else had found
the same road to Nuremberg as me
and was willing to go on record
as to all the obvious parallels
Knowing full well the raw sensitivities
of oh so many on the Right when prodded to
remember Nazi shadows,
I'd not trusted my gut
on top of which, I guess I'd forgot
the "Hakenkreuz" is nothing more
than a twisted cross
Now, let's just hope
so called inspiration doesn't strike
an eager beaver Christer balladeer
for if a kind of Kirk memorial
song and prance emerged
we'd really have some Fascist trouble on our hands.

Edgy
Charlie Berigan

Can you feel the shift?
the change, the anxiety
now a common component
to the air we breathe, the
streets we walk and the
people we see—
Each promenader starts to wonder
just who the Hell are you
Not so much with those who have been close
but absolutely true
of the many who are
strangers…
If eyes happen to hold
a gaze or glance past
instinct as to common casual
This edgy thing kicks in
and cloak of anonymity
once sacrificed to contact
isn't any help at all
For you're stuck,
kind of jailed, you see
in a prison of "us or them"
toxicity.

Maganaut Beatitudes
Charlie Berigan

Blessed are the ignorant
Favored are the blind
Lucky are the conscience free
Cursed are the kind
Knowledge is a burden, see
Decisions must be made
Take your place in MAGA land
Can't say you've not been played.

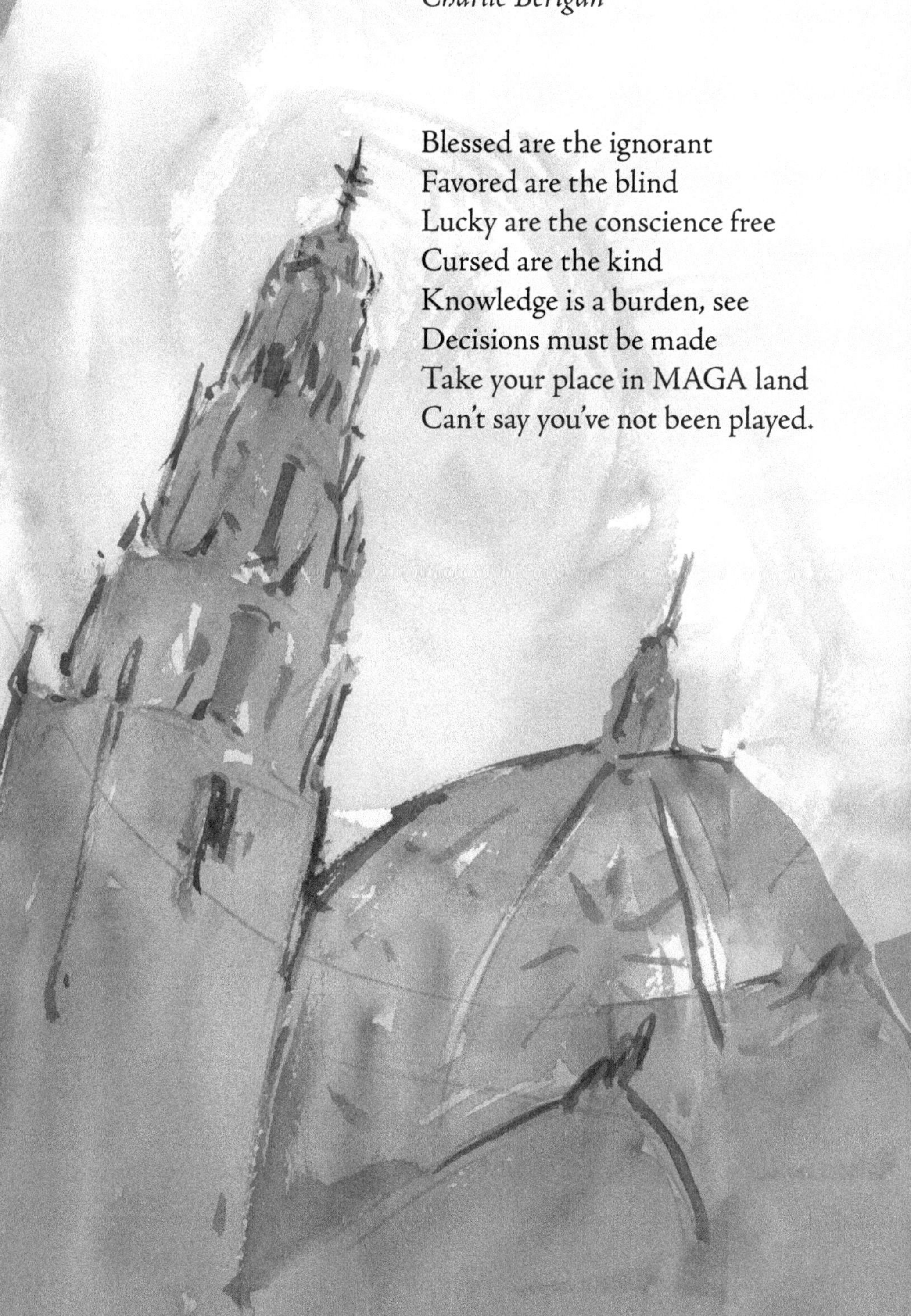

Down The Road…

Charlie Berigan

Now, just what would victory look like,
and feel like
How would we know
at last we had won?
First, a return to civility
a clear understanding
we all have a place
it's called: "human race"
Followed by crisp
recognition
difference is strength, not division
The efforts of all make
tangible merit of motto
"Out of Many, One"
And perhaps, if we're lucky
at last comprehension
greatness still beckons
We've long roads to travel
before sighting that goal
So—deep breath to start
and then, the first step.

Irene Grumman

Biography

"What are you talking about in class?" rapped my 4th Grade teacher.

"Nothing," I replied sheepishly.

"Nothing...Write a composition about nothing, and hand it in this Friday!"

I wrote about the vast nothing that separates Earth from the Sun, and keeps the planets apart. Without Nothing, everything would be all smushed together, and people would not exist.

Some of my poems rise from being confronted by a new idea; some from outrage, memories, appreciation, love. One or two a month, during the five years or so that I've been part of Sontage.

Don't Bring Dead Bodies To A Party
Irene Grumman

Don't bring dead bodies to a party.

Dead bodies laid out in rows
Shrouded in white
Like the teeth of horror
Like the grin of the war machine
Strangely artistic
Like thick bars of vertical slashes
Dotted with black clumps of mourners.

I opened my mouth in a great O.
They open their mouths in great O's
I cannot hear their shrieking.
This after-art contained on a screen
Described by a narrator.

Dead bodies will rise at this party
Amid the congratulations to the B'Mitzvah girls
Amid the love and rejoicing.

Don't bring the dead bodies of old hurts,
To this rite of passage.

Heartache Song
Irene Grumman

Broken treaties
Shattered lives
The gun
Breaks the arrow.
The arrow's
In my heart.

I love my homeland,
Not my government.
Bloodstained
Like every nation,
We decide what's fair.
What's fair is what doesn't cost
The standard of living
To which we aspire.
We value things more
Than souls,
Or each other.

My song of America
Broken promises,
Undying hope.

Cry Out

Irene Grumman

The priests had gathered, they had spoken.
"They have healed the wounds of my people lightly"
Raged the prophet.
The skin closes
Over festering wounds
Infection takes a limb
A life
A people.

The nations have gathered, they have spoken
For the first time, the sacred words
"Fossil fuels."
They make promises.
They do not keep their promises.
They vote restitution to nations which did not
    Destroy the climate
Too little. Too late.
Island nations sift sand, trying to match
    Eroding tides.

The raging young do not warn;
They cry "Disaster." They cry "Act!"
People, do not wait!
Purify. Plant. Protect.

Jon Von Erb

Biography

Poet Jon Von Erb resides in San Diego. Dubbed the poet laureate of University Heights, he mentors poets internationally online. November 2019 marked the date of his first book of poetry, Insights of a Dancing Poet. He writes poetry for the UHC newspaper, distributing his poetry free to local coffee shops as a means of giving back for a life well lived.

TACOS

With the Hands of Love upon our Faces
Jon Von Erb

by the marred candlelight of forbidden
we are forced to touch
into the dark of togetherness
our love must never see the light of discovery
for the world is cruel - free willing to cause pain,
the suffering of the innocent
like so much of this worldly existence
far too many opinions derived from hate
true love often must hide
from those who haven't an inkling as to how to love
give, accept, share
those so hard cored, so distraught by jealousy
and greed, poisoned by their own loathing
they are blinded by the innocent, the gifted
those of us that have found,
admit to and cherish the realm of love

here now I blow out the light that seeks
to confine, destroy and banish
that we might press, as one,
our lips meshed in the freedom of union,
respect and a togetherness blessed by nature
man to man, woman to woman, man to woman

Will Justice Be Served,
Is Trump To Be Indicted, Finally?

Jon Von Erb

Who Speaks

    day shines with the suns'
        bright-lightness of possibilities
    birdsongs trumpet the air
        through comfortable breezes
        cooled by Autumn's noon
    periwinkle blue skies outline
        feathered clouds of hope
    natures' confetti glitters
        the air with gilded leaves
    that tickle the human fantasy
        contentment floats in the wind

from the right   a parade pushes into the park
Nazi-esque they march westward
sudden silence engulfs
not a boot-step is heard
signs they carry   face forward
as civilian soldiers in red masks
on the backs of their heads
    strut backwards
    emotionless in march
    blue faces lost to the east

red lettered signs scream:
       'send our jobs overseas,'
          'we want dirty air, filthy water'
'ceo's should make more money'
          'tap our computer messages'
       'give free reign to industry
           without restrictions'

'pave our farmlands'
       'drill so black crude flows in rivers
      of our timber-less parks,'
    'poison us with gmo's'
'take away our health care'
      'abolish our right
        to oppose your regime'
'make our pensions pay your taxes'

with the formation disappearing into the abyss
pale faces
long and drawn
stare back
    now   we stand alone as silence deafens
    birds devoid of melody
    fold their heads into their wings of safety
    feathered clouds hang burdened with sweat
    as the sun flees to the sea
    running after the moon
    to ask her, Why?

Enough is Way Beyond Enough
Jon Von Erb

2021
was the year of the Ox. A bulldozed over year for America.
One that should have spoken a volume of warnings to
Americans to protect our nation. An unspeakable danger
lurks from within our core. An insane monster gestured while
wearing the mask of a man. A single insane non-human being.

That was the first year our nation tasted the poisoned air of
a traitor to be known as tRUMP, an insanity like never before.

Venom spewed from hellish lips that day as he ordered his
coven of snake henchmen to kill. He demanded that the
US Capital be destroyed, its legislators murdered. The fork-
tongued snake shook the nation, ordering up his planned
insurrection. His fellow misfits, thieves, and thugs almost
destroyed the Building.
With fake orange hair that bursts into flames from a corrupt
mind, he was ready to stop at nothing; his personal rampage
against American humanity.

2025

It was the year of the snake. The same serpent, now seeking
Vengeance was then voted in by a slim margin last voting day.
A single entity backed by a selfish den; the Republican party,
fooled half of our American citizens with promises they'd
never planned to keep.

The lone reptile, to this day, is still hissing and nipping
away at democracy. He's a fang-bared snake who feasted
on our pride, ate our stability, our honor, our defense,
and worse, he slivers his way toward dismantling
America's strongest institutions. Left to crumble, we lie
exposed in a hostile world. Devoid of previous strength and
an excellent global reputation, the rest of the world now pities.

2026

It is the year of the horse, nature's symbol of a strength that
gallops forth with speed and purpose. In 2025, the snake
has shed his unwanted, age-worn orange skin to face new
challenges he's set before himself. NOW is the time for the
horse to stomp on the snake in its weakest hour. NOW is
our chance to understand what has happened to America
and take steps to eradicate the harm that has befallen us.

This felonious snake has only recently felt his support
weaken. Insanity has reared its ugly head. Lies have been
discovered. Untruths harm our population. The people
who were promised a better life are ready to fight back.
A river that rages with full support shrinks to a dusty
wasteland when devoid of water. A stampede is imminent
as America is NOW prepared to reclaim our country,
reinstating democracy's strength built on respect and honor.

'News Flash'
Jon Von Erb

IN A DRAMATIC AND DISASTROUS
SUICIDE,

pages containing the 10 commandments
tore themselves,
today,
from Gideon Bibles worldwide.

Unanimous, jumping off the Cliffs of Decency
joining the Rocks of Immorality
below,

the tRUMP Newspaper gleefully
reported today.

Later, when questioned,
Gideon stated,

"Too many minds of mankind,
have evidently abandoned
humane and moral values

in favor of
returning to the
hellish pits below
the Tower of Babylon"

Imagine 2026
(our 2026's reality if we are not careful)
Jon Von Erb

Imagine there's no heaven
With tRUMP if you try
hell stings all around us
Above us, empty sky

Imagine all the people
Livin' raw, lost, alone

Imagine our torn country
It isn't hard to do
no ability to stand free
With dead religions, too

Imagine all the people
homeless and forlorn

You may say I've lost hope
And I'm not the only one
No chance someday to gain hope
For America to be as one

Imagine no security
Devoid of checks, if you can
livin' lackin' ambiguity
No brotherhood of man

Imagine all the people
Democracy deprived

You may say I'm a dreamer
And I'm not the only one
under a scheming dictator
America not living free or whole

John Lennon's
1971 Imagine

NOTE:
A dictator takes and never gives
A dictator keeps all wealth for himself
A dictator leaves his people homeless
A dictator starves his people
A dictator makes war, never peace
A dictator kills at will
A dictator rules with hate and self-desire
Beware, America, we are close to destruction
of our nation, our self-pride, respect of the world,
our freedom. It is possible if we don't wake up
and vote to keep us free with cherished rights.

In A Garden Now Devoid Of Understanding

Jon Von Erb

(Despite the horrors of our time now here in America, it is still the innocence of our children who set the perfect example, one that would lead them to protect their wheelchair bound teacher to safety despite our government's neglect to keep them safe. We live in shame, as 35% of Americans seem not to give a damn. As Ms. Cheney recently said, "tRUMP, (with this reign of hate) one day will be gone, but, the shame and scars America bears will stay with you who follow hate forever.")

As a new nation seeking all it could be, we enacted a constitution in 1787, protecting land owners, white men and, secondly, their families. It was to withstand the test of all time, holding firm through all kinds of political weather, expecting values of trust, honesty, pride and honor to endure forever. Ideas/ideals planted solely in the garden of those times. Sorely left out were considerations of women, other races, those in need, and veterans who protect us still.
Slavery was considered a white man's privilege. Well-planted rows were missing from the start. Laws of gun ownership allowed every man to own a poorly designed musket, while women's rights were not even thought of, nonetheless, planted where cultivation would keep them safe. No one, having recently escaped the unethical practices of an English king or queen and their rule, even thought that in the 2000's all aforementioned principles would now be uprooted and tossed in the garden's trash bin.

No one expected that the simple musket, designed to protect against Indians and wildlife of an undeveloped land, would turn into allowing 18-year-olds to carry sophisticated military weaponry in the 2000's. Everyone knew that to purchase a gun meant that that person expected to use it. No one knew we'd elect Reagan, an unprincipled man, into office, a man who closed mental facilities, thus now being deemed the father of American Homelessness. Who could foretell the selfishness of a party that has done all it can to bulldoze democracy out of existence?

Who could have foretold a party that cares more about owning a gun than they do in keeping our children safe and alive? Could a simple God-fearing/respecting 1700's person even conceive that in this era religion would be used as a weapon against decency? And who today doesn't look at this horror, our garden, we have all but destroyed?

Aren't we in constant mental and ethical pain, currently witnessing the death of a sovereign and loving nation, one whose founders stole America from Indian Americans who welcomed us once as visitors to their land? Who today doesn't realize how our once beautiful garden existence, is now destined to be a lifeless, barren field of thorns, burrs, and dust?

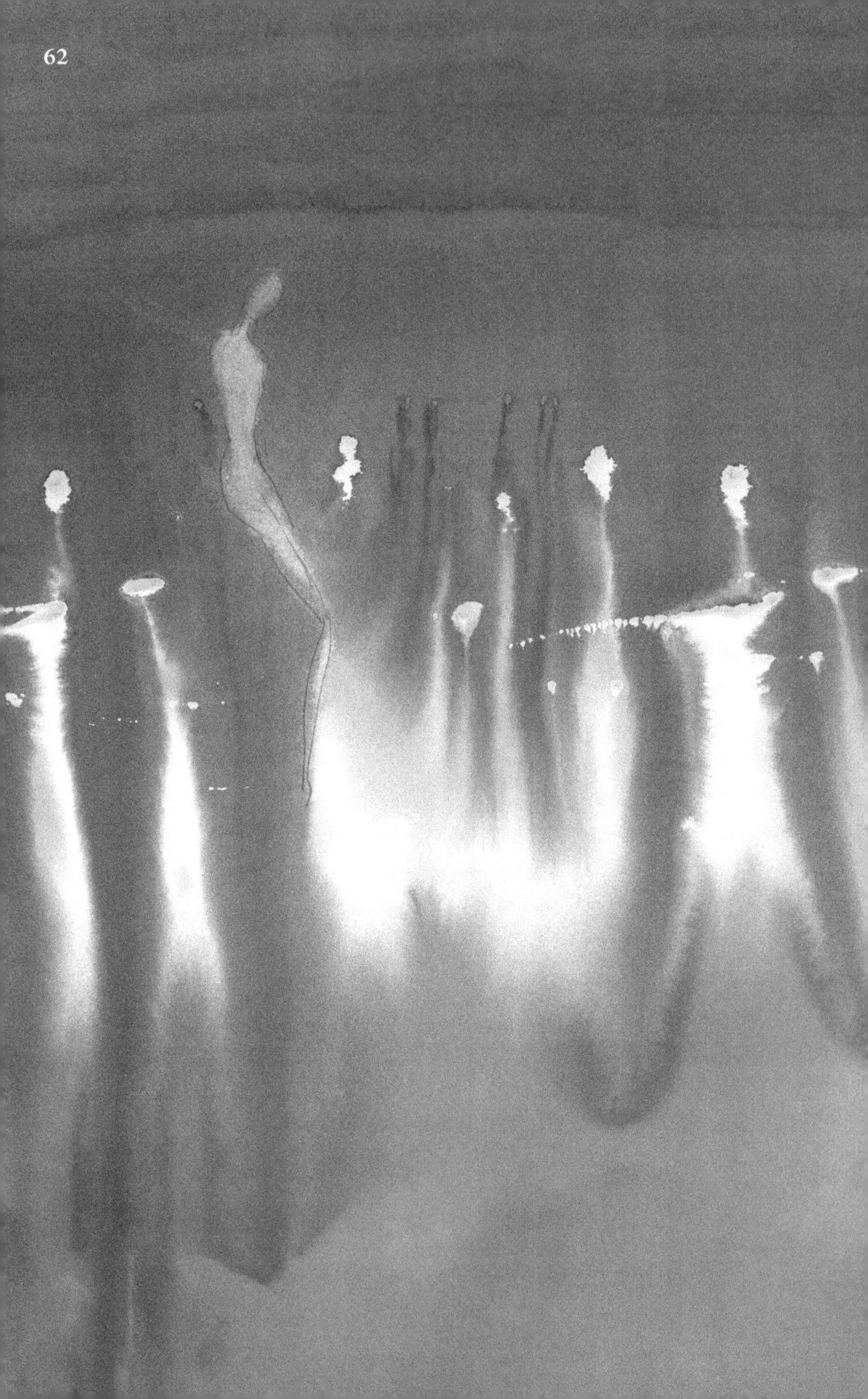

Michael Turner-Ortega

Biography

Born in San Luis Obispo California long distance runner since childhood, U. S. Navy flight deck crew member from '75 to '79 with numerous Phonological experiences to share.

Can't Help But Think About It
Michael Turner-Ortega

on a fundamental Carrier frequency
because everything is related
on the
        different plains
everywhere
         on the level
by the highway
drawn to a holy fountain
made by our sacred mother
 in an aquifer full of love
a meaningful existence
         on many levels
with a sanctified code
     to honor all beings
running down the road to
       connectedness
to no place in particular
      or even live on in a
purposeful life
     making joyful noise
and playing fair authentically
the fountain continues to
flow
         never ends
overwhelms
      the right place
the right time

Refined Focus
Michael Turner-Ortega

looking back into the past makes us flow
into the future with a strong sense fleeting
moments in   lived experience
pure information without   bias
intent is a force in the universe
what really happens when we remember
things that have never taken place
it's in this inner-self that gets expressed
because thoughts are things and things
are so existential at the same time
on many levels   save my spot
its all verifiable in the scheme of things
what has been and what will be
events that have made mark with a strong
sense of fleeting moments at four o'clock
in the afternoon somewhere
you could put all the rest of it aside
wherever it belongs in-between time
large birds jump up and down entertain me
and the smallish horse beside me smiles

Generated Fusion
Michael Turner-Ortega

this might have been a tragic story   withdrawn
willing to entertain the idea of happiness
and how I made it out alive sometimes it's
easy to ignore at a distance with a cloudbank
closing in   around the sound of generated
fusion   crossing the threshold of another
lifetime   walking around the idea of living
life without any reference   not being allowed
to mourn in a visible way
in the anatomy fractured intent
a beautiful memory gets hidden with suppressed
melancholy under winter stars out on a cold
night without any clouds   infinite space makes
its way home   and for those of you who have
made a connection to this – well good for you –
who's gonna know what side you're on anyway
upturned against the curb
how mysterious those thoughts are   that are
bundled together instead of separate

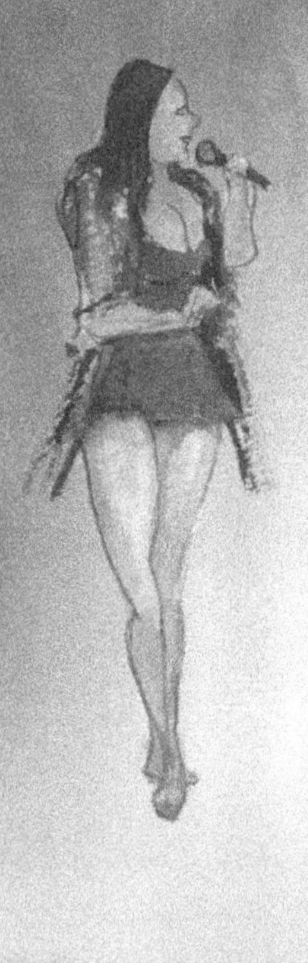

The Bigger Picture
Michael Turner-Ortega

out of nowhere   a voice begins to speak
opens with   "as ever for now"   shuts
the front door   over and over again
surrounded by uncertainty   a broken
america weaves itself into a bundle of
sweetgrass   made me feel both
dark and light together as everything
disappears
up in arms with the voice of reason
people with hate in their heart rise up
kinder people rise up and spread the love
with something to think about in the
language of their bone songs that
become footprints walking through ashes
of grief
something greater forms around each
others hears   us and them
become one family
ashes become bricks to build bridges
with
we become on voice wildflowers
bloom in a celebration of life
delivers a brighter future
within a multitude of generations
nothing is insignificant
    in the bigger picture

Down Right Peppy
Michael Turner-Ortega

oh joy   oh bother   free will
justifies illumination as separation
unified experiences above ground
under the tide   movement
thrown into the dumpster of
enlightenment
the mail didn't come today and
that's alright   a mind all cluttered
up the way it's supposed to be with
eyes full of gratitude   no worries
the day lingers on   in a hurried
kind of way
simplified
fabricated experience on
its way out   willful magnitude
shows up in a flash
just witnessed a wrong name to my
right   don't tell anyone who it was
laughter's the only way out with
no place to go
unashamed
remorse
looks the other way   because
there's no place to go anyhow

Susan D. Walter

Biography

Susan, born in Texas (but escaped at age 2), was raised in Southern California. She arrived in San Diego County with her boyfriend Ken, who was driving his Mach One Mustang. The Mustang was towing Susan's Corvair, which also carried 2 huge angelfish in a bucket, her black cat Goblin, and two guinea pigs Shiloh and Gretchen. Our lunch break in Oceanside resulted in irrepressible giggles when the piggies yeeped, startling everyone who walked by.

Susan married someone else after college, they have two adult children, and she has recently retired from being a historic archaeologist in San Diego County. She has too many hobbies.

Little known fact: As a child, Susan wanted to be a mermaid when she grew up - Luckily, she changed her mind.

The Daily Spew – Project 2025
Susan D. Walter

Which one, I ask you, of the year 2025's daily spew
Has reached the bottom of disgust for you?
He boasts, brags, lies, mumbles the same tired crap – and never shuts up:
I imagine t-RUMP's words and thoughts…

How I *love* those money bags that bought my election!
Put Obama in jail!
Jail Hillary!
Kamala is a moron!
Biden? He's just an autopen – the worst president in American history.
I'm a genius!
And I am above the law!
All those January 6th criminals – I can pardon them!
Other creeps I can pardon too.
Oh yes how nice the Supreme Court and gop all support me!
Birthday parade for me, me, me! Complete with military flyover!
Let's go to Mars!
I'll fix Russia and Ukraine's issues immediately!
Greenland! We need it, they should realize that! We'll get it!
The DOGE will get rid of waste and woke spending.
I could be Pope!
I should be on Mount Rushmore!
Of *course,* there are only male and female – and we'll make *that* law, too.
Oh yes, I can give power to my cronies and supporters; the Department of
Education, Head of Navy, help
from my pal the Postmaster General? They can learn the ropes on the job. They
can pay *me* for it!
Gold Trump cards, purchased for $5,000,000 will give you an expedited chance
for American citizenship!
Hey – did you buy a great Tesla from the capitol lawn?
Who cares if the East Wing was part of a National Register structure that
belongs to the people of this
country? It is *mine* to do with *what I want to.*

Have you reserved your place in *my* soon to be built ballroom?
How's your collection of trading cards? Need a bunch, or just a few?
Gaza? Who cares? I'll just bomb a few Venezuelan ships as diversion; floating survivors are fun to shoot!
Poor, poor, heroic Charlie Kirk; let's canonize him!
So what if Rob Reiner's murdered – he wouldn't ever vote for me, and no talent either.
And there's the never ending drama of Epstein – what a sexpot playboy I am and always have been!
And check out my elegant redecoration of the White House in gold!
So proud of my video dumping *shit* on American citizens!
And showing Obama in jail!
Oh, don't forget my revisionist history on the plaques of the Presidential Hallway! And the White House website!
With *me* head of Kennedy Center, culture will flourish!
We need battleships! Maybe even 40 of them!
Thank God I can send the National Guard to quell those useless dissidents!
And with the fabulous help of ICE I can deport *anyone!*

And I show my American pride for deporting all those immigrants! The goal is 1,000 per day!
Where's *my* Nobel Prize? For peace?
If you don't love me, you are sick with Trump Derangement Syndrome!
And be sure you buy Melania's lovely Christmas ornaments…
Branding opportunities galore!

This spew is but my view
of what's happened since Election '25
No doubt this lout
Has had his fun
Sadly, the story's far from done.

Bottomless disgust for me and you…

Conflict on the Sidewalk
Susan D. Walter

I spied her about 200 feet away, while walking my
frisky dog
As we approached the tiny elderly woman
I pulled my nosy pet in with a stern "Heel, Asmar."
Obediently, she did.

My usual friendly greeting froze, unsaid.
I now saw the red letters T R U M P on the cap on
her head
And the Make America Great Again across her
skinny chest.
Repulsed, I was.

My day was now clouded with disgust
Destroyed by her clothing that she used to cuss
I wanted to huff "You are deluded"
I did not.

In this country you can still express your opinion
It was clear on her face she enjoyed my mistrust
Her face exhibited t-RUMP triumph
Her grin so ugly.

I guess she thought she'd won.
I'd moved aside for her
I did not challenge her
She strutted.

An Afghan Bites a Carrot
Susan D. Walter

So satisfying to all – but perhaps not the carrot:

The carrot was viewed with skepticism.
By the Afghan.
A cautious sniff.
Her paw bats at it.

The Afghan looked carefully, noting, perhaps, just odd
shading?
Dogs don't see color do they?
It is orange with a bright green top.

The Afghan circled around it.
Maybe this is the back?
Is this where to attack?

Creep…crouch…
Pounce!
Chomp!
Chew chew chew chew…
Drop this thing.
Pounce!
Toss this thing in the air!

The Afghan tips her head.
It doesn't move.
It must be dead.
Boring thing…
Stupid thing.

But will it revive?
Be again alive?
In 2025?

Who else will survive?
Project 2025:
Other Afghans are hung out to dry.
By another carrot.

California At Half Mast*
Susan D. Walter

Beasts prowl our country
slavering for power and money.
The law of the land is ignored and
      our laws are broken at will.

Beasts, did I say?
      Oh what a mistake:
Our true beasts are dying in droves
      as land that they need
      to feed and to breed
is raped for its resource's gold.

Humans suffer and scream:
wicked ICE is deployed
to jobs, courts, and homes
      or the street.

People dragged off, incarcerated
      for nothing wrong they have done.
Some are sent to terrible danger
      families separated.

And we here in California
      the liberal land of sunshine and dreams?
We resist your ravening greed:
      You won't make us submit to you, we're true
Democratic blue!

We're brown, we are black, we are white,
        and yellow, and red, and blends.
We all of us proudly declare
        "We're free and you can't change our
beliefs: go back, wretch, and hide in your
lair."

I saw the symbol of us:
        The federal flag was not there.
Our grizzly bear triumphantly flew
        but at half mast; we grieve it is
there.

Oh say can you see
        Hope: OUR triumph will be
YOUR library should burn to the ground
        so no vestige of you creeps around
and you disappear in anonymity.

Then patriots true Americans like me
can be found
celebrating our country's return to
        kindness, law, and democracy.

My Flags
Susan D. Walter

I like my colored banners waving in the breezes
At the bottom of the pole is blue and yellow
for poor Ukraine's misery
Next up is a rainbow backing the California grizzly
bear
Above that is my beloved green white and black Peace
flag
Above, at the top is…
      I'll get to that.

On my huge podocarpus tree is a flag of the blue
marble
– our Earth –
Against the fence is black, blue and white
      COEXIST to celebrate religious freedom
Hanging from the central pole of my tent frame is…
      I'll get to that.

Now.
These two other flags are bright red, white and blue.
Yes, this country's prideful banners.
One with 50 stars, the other with thirteen in a circle.
They are both sad.
Upside down.
      I got to that.

Too Much
Susan D. Walter

My complaint of problems and politics
Written in the car on my way to Sontage

It was midnight
		Weak and weary
I pondered lack of sleep
		I'm weary

Shoulder, hips
		My friend is hurt
And I am crusty
		With lots of dirt

Managed to feed em all
		My pets
Gulped some coffee
Took a shower
Did what I could
In my power

I'm so angry
		Out of touch
There is so much
		Too much too much

But now I know
Because of sleaze
I'm suffering from
		"Functional freeze"

Daily things
		Impossible to deal
The daily spew
		Won't let me heal

This is why
		Dear Sontage crew
This stupid rhyme
I've writ for you.

Mary Magdalene Ardagna

Biography

Her given name is Mary Magdalene Ardagna, so it was probably inevitable that she would be magical, mystical, and somewhat misunderstood. In her youth, she studied Economics at Bryn Mawr College and later, Goju Karate in Central Park. Gap-toothed like the Wife of Bath, with a fondness for felines and fancy rocks, Mary happily spends her retirement in her fairy garden, listening to the wind dancing through the many chimes to serenade her.

God's Children
Mary Magdalene Ardagna

I heard that
Christmas
Was canceled
In Jerusalem
This year
Because
God's children
Can't
Get
Along

Life in These Times
Mary Magdalene Ardagna

I keep my vision very small these days
It seems to work out for the best that way
The world is so full of so many things
Some highly improbable just a few short months ago
Yet now they populate
This new reality
Where the old rules don't apply
And no new rules have yet
Moved in to take their place
Everything is suspended
And replaced with disbelief

But here in my garden
I plant the seeds of love
And water the tiny fragile sprouts
Coaxing them to grow

Fuck Andrew Cuomo

Mary Magdalene Ardagna

*Note: I know the other side of our history and am
choosing to ignore it for the purposes of this poem.*

Today I can feel a change a-coming
All across this great land of ours
People turned out to vote in record numbers
For ourselves and our neighbors
The poor the hungry the immigrants
Remembering the history
Of our country
Born from the blood, sweat and tears
Of those who left shores
Where they didn't fit in
In search of a freedom they didn't possess

Born from a rebellion by those
Who threw tea into a harbor in protest
And took up arms against an unjust system of
government

Perhaps we are remembering that
We the people
Hold the power

Perhaps the dinosaur democrats
Will remember or learn that
With great power comes great responsibility
Not to lobbyists, shareholders, corporations, each
other
But responsibility to us
The people
We put them into office and we can take them out.
Any day now.

Shoveling Shit
Mary Magdalene Ardagna

So much of life comes down to shoveling shit

Shoving papers around at a job
Filling files with memos no one ever reads
Whether paper or now digital
The files pile up into mountains
The emails pile up until there are pages and pages
Hundreds, thousands, tens of thousands
Too many to read
Or even delete
And more just keep on coming
Day after day
Hour by hour
Minute by minute
Complete inundation

Everything you buy
Everything you do
Lands you on another list
Review this product
Sign this petition

Not to mention
The political propaganda
Flooding the airwaves
And the inbox
One must be armed
With hip waders
And discernment
To maintain any balance
And not be bowled over

Sometimes literal shit is almost a relief
Taking care of a friend's big dogs
Petting and loving
Feeding -- oh no
Feeding leads to shoveling
Pile after pile of shit
Some dry, some still steaming
Some in between
Get on that damn shovel
You squishy turd
Sometimes it falls back on the grass
Or slides onto the ground
instead of into the bucket

Shoveling horse shit is way less unpleasant
There's more of it but
Way less smelly

Give me a cat litter box instead
At least it's more confined
Not like chasing poop around the backyard

Cleaning cat litter boxes
Used to be my least favorite task
Until I had to shovel dog shit
Who knew

Misogynistic Propaganda
Mary Magdalene Ardagna

It's always the woman's fault
Ever since Eve gave Adam the apple
What about the snake?
The mother always caused all the neurosis
What about the dad?
He wasn't there enough to share
In the upbringing or bear
Any of the responsibility

If someone behaves badly towards a woman
What did she do to cause it?
What did she say? Or wear?

All my life I heard that
It's the females' fault
They are the ones who cause
All the trouble
Now you tell me male mosquitoes
Also suck out our life's blood
Maybe it's possible the rest of that stuff
Isn't all our fault either

Just another
Whiskey Girl

86 47
Mary Magdalene Ardagna

I really miss the days
When he was just
A sleazy businessman
With an oversized ego
The short-fingered vulgarian
As per Spy magazine

A slumlord
A shyster
Racist
Unethical
A blowhard
Corrupt

Too full of himself
To even realize
He was the butt
Of the joke

I watched his TV vanity project
Out of nostalgia for New York City
And to marvel at
His ability
To take himself seriously

I never thought so many people
Who swore
To uphold the constitution
Would abdicate their responsibility

I guess the joke's on me

☙ The Last Word ❧

Mark	Hopefully this isn't it
Karen	Let's keep creating no matter what. Stay connected to the people you love and care about. And follow Joseph Goldstein's counsel to act on a generous impulse the moment it arises.
Brian	in fighting evil / to defeat evil we must be / we must embody — we will become it / more than its fiction / its contradiction
Charlie	"Someday, this war's gonna end… 'cause DONALD DON'T SURF!!!"
Irene	Listening to the poetry of others inspires and moves me. Thank you, Sontage, for laughs, surprises and wonders.
Jon	Positivity will win over negativity every time. One guesses what one can be positive about in these political times. I say what goes up goes down eventually. I just hope that we aren't drowned in the process. Positivity wins the day, every day.
Michael	Communicates with my Ancestors who need to share their lived experience through me.
Susan	I got a new dog! And, guess what? She is very opinionated. Everyone should speak out!
Mary	Love is the answer to every question.